SUZANNE KASLER
SOPHISTICATED SIMPLICITY

SUZANNE KASLER
SOPHISTICATED SIMPLICITY

RIZZOLI
NEW YORK

New York · Paris · London · Milan

To Martha and Jim

Contents

Introduction

Ihave a passion for houses. And I have always loved creating homes in my mind and then translating them into reality. Whenever I wonder where this comes from, I think about my parents and grandparents, who have always inspired me. It is funny how life unfolds. I grew up in a military family. We moved every two years, which meant we did not have the kind of childhood home that you spend your entire young life in. Yet every summer my parents, my sister, Nanette, and brother, Jim, who are twins, and I would go to stay with my father's parents at their home in Indiana. Their house was full of collections. My grandparents had a passion for antiques, so they would take me to the local antiques shows. My grandmother made quilts, and she loved china. Every summer when we visited, my memories from previous summers would surface. I think these experiences are where my deep desire to make the kind of home that creates family memories comes from. These houses can be any type or size, so long as they express their owner's personality and style, and feel at home in their location. They can be in town, or in the country, or at the shore.

My mother and father, Martha and James H. Kasler, taught me by example that whatever happens, if you stay positive and make the best of things, it is possible to keep moving forward. My father was a fighter pilot in the United States Air Force, and he

The Wonder Years

was a prisoner of war in Vietnam for seven years. When he came home, he shared his story. What was especially interesting to me was that during his time in the Hanoi Hilton, he was designing a golf course in his mind. Not only did my father have this incredible career journey, he was also what is called a "pilot's pilot." Pilots loved him. He inspired them. He thought of them. My mother was just as influential. And she has always stayed optimistic, no matter what. When my father came home, he told me, "never lose your spirit." I have always remembered this.

After my father retired from the Air Force, he and my mother bought a golf course in Illinois. And over the next several years, he created this beautiful country golf course, hole by hole. What this inspired in me was the belief that having a passion for something, and being positive about it, can translate into reality. This is one of the great gifts my parents gave me. For designers, the process of creating a home can be described just that simply. We envision it in our minds. And we stay the course.

As I began working on my third book, what kept resonating with me is how much more my clients know about good design today. I have come to realize that the people who hire designers really appreciate design. I have also seen that they are focused on a more edited, more modern, fresher approach to design—what I think of as sophisticated simplicity.

Being able to design homes that create memories for our clients is so special. The experiences we share with them along the way become a part of their story, as well as the story of their home. As we look at things together, we help them discover their own style. We always find that one special thing that inspires our design process and everything that follows. Once we do, we gradually develop the concept and work together to create rooms that will reflect who they are and how and where they live. It can be a challenge to find

Homecoming

just the right furnishings, art, and objects to express their personalities. These pieces have to capture their lifestyle and the spirit of the place. That is why when we find them, it is also the greatest joy.

I am always looking for beauty—for what is chic, what is pretty, and what is refined—for new ideas about style, and for fashion that is timely, but timeless, too. Sometimes the simplest things give me great pleasure. Sometimes I am surprised by what captures my heart and sparks my imagination. I find that travel inspires me the most. As a designer, being inspired is everything. It is the gift I've been given. It is why I am always out looking. And it is what I want to bring to each client. As I watch our world evolve, I am excited about the easy access that all of us who love design now have to everything from everywhere. Yet this unlimited access, as wonderful as it is, can also be overwhelming because with it comes the huge pressure of too much choice. So I find my clients come to me today for my edited approach—and for the sophisticated simplicity that I bring to their homes.

INSPIRED

Designers are unique in that we can design for ourselves. But once we finish our own houses, we need places to showcase all we truly want to express. That's why I love doing show houses, showrooms, and vignettes. Each is a new opportunity for me to push the envelope and to inspire others. That's what I think continues to create style.

I am a collector. And I love so many different things. I constantly experiment and search for the right mix of furnishings and objects—high and low; antique, vintage and modern; the latest ideas from fashion and design—to capture the spirit of a place and the essence of a personality. Show houses and showrooms are welcome challenges. I am always inspired to try different ways of putting things together, and new color and finish combinations.

Some show houses are fancier than others. A few years ago, I was asked to be a part of the Kips Bay Decorator Show House, America's premier show house, in New York City. Our room had some unique spatial challenges, among them a lowered ceiling that cut in at no logical place and could not be elevated. We were also next to the kitchen, the terrace, and a hallway. I finally chose to lacquer the whole room in a high-gloss white paint, and wrap it in a fluted molding trim the exact height of the bulkhead. After we carefully layered in some of our most favorite beautiful things, we realized we had named the room just right: Sophisticated Simplicity.

Our Kips Bay Decorator Show House room presented us with several architectural challenges:
a partially dropped ceiling that divided the room asymmetrically, and three ways to enter the room.
To simplify the architecture, we lacquered everything white and bleached the French oak wood
floors. This allowed us to layer in sophisticated elements, new and old, and many found objects.

From the antique chairs, contemporary upholstery, and vintage parchment coffee table to the petite side tables from the Paris Flea Market, we did the entire room in gorgeously textured neutrals, accented by a palette of whispery colors introduced by the antique rug. The contemporary bookcase allowed me to mass many of my collections, which is how I love to bring in a personal touch. The vintage columns picked up the fluting of our added moldings. So does the painting by Dusty Griffith, one of my very favorite artists.

When I talk about sophisticated simplicity, I am talking about the challenge of editing. The whole point of designing a room in a show house or a showroom is to inspire. That allows me to really challenge myself and explore ideas that I might not have tried before.

Show houses are always meant to inspire—and Kips Bay is especially about that. But in order to inspire others, you have to be inspired yourself. As a designer, I stay inspired by being out and about, looking at beauty wherever I find it—in antiques shops, in the details of fashion and jewelry, in retail spaces. Whenever I travel to another city, or to Europe, or even to a cute store in Atlanta, I am always collecting items that end up in the spaces I design. And I use them because they are my favorite things.

Because this wall was between the kitchen and a hallway, we couldn't put furniture along it. I decided to hang these fabulous mirrors by Mark Evans, a San Francisco artist. I'd purchased one after another for myself over several years, and all of a sudden I had a collection. Though I worried about whether it would be enough, everyone loved it.

The Atlanta Homes & Lifestyles Southeastern
Designer Showhouse gave me the opportunity
to try something I'd never done before.
Usually, I use a lot of color in a dining room.
And I often paint the ceiling a metallic shade
of oyster. Here, I did almost the reverse,
matching the fabrics to the gorgeous French
gray-blue shade of the ceiling, from Fine Paints
of Europe. I love giving dining room chairs a
whitewashed finish so they don't distract from
the table, especially when, as here, it's a dark
wood. Paul Ferrante made the Russian-inspired
chandelier, the only one of its kind.

I have discovered that when I buy the things I love, they always end up being a unique part of one of my designs. In this show house dining room, a collection of twenty-eight geometric white plaster moldings, which I couldn't resist when I saw them in Paris, finally found their perfect home.

When you are asked to be the honorary chair of the Atlanta Homes & Lifestyles Southeastern Designer Showhouse, it is a privilege to be proud of. I selected the dining room because its lofty proportions appealed to me, as did the ceiling's unusual beam detail. While I was thinking about what to do, I found a linen velvet and a silk taffeta in a gorgeous shade of French gray blue. These fabrics inspired me to try something completely new for a dining room: to lacquer all the walls in white, and the ceiling panels in the same French gray blue. The effect was a wonderful surprise for someone who almost always uses lots of color in a dining room. And it made the collections within stand out in sharp detail.

When we started the room, I thought I would wallpaper it. At one point, I even debated using wallpaper on the ceiling because of the huge panels between the beams. In the end, I decided to use chinoiserie panels as art to reference the wallpaper idea—and because they're beautiful.

Twice a year people come from all over the world to the High Point Market in North Carolina. When I introduce my new collections for Hickory Chair there, I want to present people with fresh ideas. With each showroom space I create for them, I want to try new things. This is a large part of my inspired world.

Even though this showroom space seems to include just as much black as it does white—as if the two shades are in perfect balance—there are really only a few black elements: some pottery, a throw, a few strategically placed pillows, and the pom-pom Moroccan blanket, which is so graphic and whimsical. I think the result proves again how any color stands out more when it is surrounded by white. I love the simplicity of the palette. And I love the mixture of high with low, of rustic with refined. To me, the combination is very sophisticated and fun.

We saw this pom-pom Moroccan blanket at Creel and Gow on a trip to New York. I couldn't stop thinking about it, and began to wonder about using it in the showroom. Once we got in to set up, we discovered a large column behind the spot where we wanted to place the sofa. The blanket fits there perfectly. And everyone ended up loving it as much as I do.

SUZANNE KASLER TIMELESS STYLE

SAIL *MAJESTY AT SEA* DREW DOGGETT

When we're finishing up a project, we'll go out looking for the last few pieces. We know we'll always find a few that are really special. When we do, it feels like they've been waiting for us all along.

Each season, we are in a different area within the Hickory Chair showroom. Our location plays a large role in what I decide to do with the color palette and the finishes. During this market, we were showcasing the pieces in an industrial building with steel windows and wood beams. We decided to take our cues from the simplicity and strength of the architecture, and to do everything in black and white. The bold, graphic palette showcased my furniture designs really well. I think it was also inspiring to the people who visited because black and white always looks fresh. It gives anyone with an eye for design unexpected ideas about how to rethink things. The hope to inspire is why we do these kinds of projects, and why they give us creative energy and freedom.

PRECEDING SPREAD: The architecture sets the tone for our casual, elegant mix. OPPOSITE: I came across this black painting in Paris. It wasn't expensive, and it had a few cracks. Everyone who knows how much I love color was surprised by how attracted I was to it. But there's such strength in its simplicity, and it has ended up being a great backdrop.

TOWN

I love doing houses in town. They're usually the main residence, so I want them to reflect their owners' personal style and also their geographic location. If people have traveled, if they've accumulated art, books, and objects, we'll include their collections here. Often these houses have a more dressed-up feel, even when they're casually elegant. But no matter what, my key is to make them really comfortable— and really beautiful.

Belle Meade

I have always believed that the best homes look like the people who live in them. So for every client—and each phase of life—I work to find unique, appropriate solutions. Sometimes, the challenge focuses just on design and decoration. Sometimes, as with this young, Nashville-based family of five, it involves creating both a look and a lifestyle.

They had just moved back from Bermuda to be close to their families when I met them. After living in a two-hundred-year-old house on the island, they knew and loved the sensibility of history, but didn't want to be weighed down by it. The home they had just purchased in Nashville, a twenty-year-old Georgian-style manor set amid gorgeous gardens and grounds, was clad in the most beautiful gray stone, which made it look like it was original to the neighborhood.

They asked for a home that felt relevant, young, and more modern—and full of color—but that still had a foundation of tradition. Architect Heather Francis Robers and I revised the interior architecture, which lacked the details that create character. Landscape architect Ben Page reenvisioned the gardens and grounds. In my experience, if you can get the architecture right, you can do less decorating. This is part of the magic that helps make rooms feel timeless and of their time.

PAGE 33: I often take my clients shopping for antiques when we begin working on a new project. When we found this eighteenth-century painted Swedish commode, we fell in love with its color and patina. And it started everything. OPPOSITE: Often we can fix the architecture by stripping away excess ornament and detail. Here, we did the reverse, adding classic moldings to the rooms to give them a framework of formality and history. The bold panel details in the entry hall set the stage. I used the stunning Italian period settee to begin the story of how the house unfolds.

I believe a home should have a sense of place. In part, that means making sure the inside and the outside relate to each other. So I am always thinking about—and looking for cues in—the surrounding context. One of my favorite things about this house was the warm gray stone of its exterior, which had such subtle variations of tone and texture. I decided to pull that gray inside to use with shades of taupe and white as the basis for the fabric palette. And then fold in variations of the owner's favorite color, aubergine—and some lovely blues for contrast.

ABOVE: This is my favorite stone house. It reminds me of the English countryside. OPPOSITE: When you come into the house, you look straight through the living room out to the gardens and grounds beyond. I waited to paint the side entry to the living room in lavender until the very end, because it's such a statement. Often I'll take a small space that's adjacent a larger room and paint it a signature color because that color will refer back to other parts of the house where the color occurs. This is the way I use color strategically, because most of the houses we do are in whites, bones, and creams. The distinctive moldings here bring each room into sharp focus. The rug's subtle textures contrast with the wonderfully carved consoles, which are overscale and an interesting surprise.

We carefully edited the mix of periods and styles here so that each plays to and off the others. The antique mirror is almost like an art piece because it's all alone on that wall. Along with the oversize consoles and a pair of Jansen bergères, they establish a foundation of elegance that speaks to a very European lifestyle. In a tonal palette like this, strong accents—the aubergines and blue grays—layer in interest without overwhelming. We upholstered the sofa in a blue velvet inspired by the Swedish commode. The Greek key band that finishes the edge of the drapes is one of those details that adds quiet sophistication.

RIGHT: It's interesting to me as a designer that when the time is right, we find just the right thing. That's when it feels as if the piece has been waiting for us. We came across this fabulous eighteenth-century Gustavian wallpaper screen at Lief, an antiques store, on a shopping trip to Los Angeles and decided to frame it and hang it as an artwork in the living room. It inspired so many of our fabrics. After we had finished the project and the client had been living in the house, we went to the Antiques and Garden Show of Nashville. Much to our surprise, we found just the right pair of elongated antique benches. One fit perfectly in the space below the screen. The other we placed at the top of the landing. FOLLOWING SPREAD: The mix of new and old creates a room that is collected. The eighteenth-century French limestone mantel layers another Continental reference into the composition. I love the way it looks with contemporary art by Dusty Griffith.

With color, as with many aspects of design, the right balance is everything. The velvet on the dining chairs, and a console with fabric custom dyed in Italy with accents in the same hue, add complexity to the aubergine story. Platinum silk on the walls infuses the room with warmth, sophistication, and an understated sheen. To strengthen the architecture, we finished the simplicity of the walls with a beautiful molding.

Aubergine is such a strong statement that we wanted to make sure we used it throughout the house in a timeless way. The dining room is the one place where we felt free to use a more saturated color. Touches of silver leaf add glamour. We then dressed the room down with a sisal rug banded in velvet.

ABOVE: One of the challenges of this dining room was its large size. We had to include enough pieces of furniture to make it appear collected and unique. I love using skirted consoles. They give you a chance to bring in a custom printed fabric, which adds a lot of dimension to the room. The modern mirror creates a wonderful juxtaposition with the early nineteenth-century Italian chandelier. OPPOSITE: From the beginning, we focused on acquiring contemporary art. The painting by Steven Seinberg found its perfect place on this dining room wall. It continues the story of overscale pieces that make you appreciate everything happening in the room.

We created the architectural envelope here by painting the walls, ceiling, and trim all the same shade and finish of bone white. The addition of the steel-and-glass doors made the flow between the indoors and outdoors completely organic. The planter and the sculptural limestone ball add surprise.

48

Because the family room was so large, we wanted to create separate, cozy areas to hang out. Again, inspired by our antiques shopping, we found a fabulous antique Italian bookcase to anchor the room. We tucked a custom banquette into the corner for doing homework, sitting and working on a puzzle, or even having a casual family meal. Our clients love how we put together collections. By starting this wall with a collage of found pieces, we've inspired them to keep collecting.

Our most significant decisions in the family room were architectural. We wanted to open up this space to interact with the exterior and make it more modern, so we replaced the existing traditional, arched wooden windows with a wall of high, steel-and-glass French doors. Now the inside and outside connect seamlessly.

We painted the family room a warm shade of bone that emphasizes the crispness of the architectural detail and that glows ethereally when the sun streams in. Natural linen, taupe velvets, and accents of blue—this palette comes from the muted Oushak. The panels over the fireplace pivot back to reveal the television. We widened the entry to the kitchen to connect the two rooms.

The owners have three young children, so we wanted to give them a kitchen that would serve all their needs. Light-filled and comfortable, this room is definitely the heart of the house. I love that by keeping the architectural envelope white—white trim, white doors, and white ceiling—it creates a more edited background. Painting the walls the most muted gray-blue makes the white stand out even more.

ABOVE: In a family house, I think one of the most important rooms is the back hall mudroom. It often gets overlooked. Here, we turned the mudroom into a space with a secret by hiding all the storage for the children's things behind the paneling. We even added another piece of contemporary art. OPPOSITE: At the same time, I love having the classic console, mirror, and lamp that you leave on at night so you don't walk into a dark house.

I have always loved seeing small, unexpected moments of color. They pique your interest and tie the rooms of a house together in a way that makes emotional sense. To tell the story of the palette further here, we painted an intimate porch that connects the living room to the master bedroom in lavender. It reflects, in a subtle way, the colors that unfold in the house.

Buckhead

Every house we work on with our clients is a labor of love, but some, like this one, are even more so. This couple is truly passionate about architecture and design. He received a master's in architecture from Georgia Tech and used to be on the faculty there. She is a lawyer with a passion for interior design. When they found this 1927-era house on two acres in Atlanta's Buckhead neighborhood, it was in very sad shape, a real faded beauty. They wanted to restore it in a historically authentic way, down to the last molding. Along with Atlanta-based architects Spitzmiller & Norris and landscape architect Graham Pittman, we have done that, bringing it vividly back to life after taking it down to the studs, adding onto its original footprint, and transforming the backyard with cutting and kitchen gardens and a series of other outdoor destinations.

The house has an unusual kind of delicacy about it that is just so pretty. But it is very small in square footage. We had to make sure the rooms flowed physically and visually from one to the next. The challenge for us was the scale and making it live in the way you want a house to live today.

PAGE 61: Painted the palest of pale ice blues, the new side entrance practically dissolves in the light. OPPOSITE: Instead of a black and white floor, we decided on Bulgarian limestone for a quiet elegance. Window coverings would have obscured the architectural details, so we introduced fabric with the skirted table on the room's other side.

They are Renaissance people, with grown children. He is a gourmet chef. She is a serious cook. They garden. She sews. They love to entertain. Their shelves hold a thousand books—and they have read them all. She has all of her favorite things. With such beautiful architecture—and such intimate spaces—it was really important to edit with great restraint. We did that, and the house speaks to their needs. But it is also chic, fresh, and design appropriate. Most of all, it entertains amazingly for groups small and very large, as they have discovered. Today we all think we must have large houses, but a more intimate place like this is so effortlessly livable it could change our minds.

OPPOSITE: The house's front door opens from the front porch directly into the living room. This presented a real design challenge. That's why we added the side entrance. ABOVE: When the architects restored the house, which dates to approximately 1927 and was one of the first in the neighborhood, they reintroduced the columns that were original to the front entry.

The owners love the foundation of tradition and beautiful design, but they wanted their rooms to be stylish and relevant for today, so we collected the pieces for the living room with that in mind. The pair of gold tables is in keeping with the architecture and their gold dining room chandelier. The antique mirrors add a graphic element to the subtle colors.

With limited floor and wall space—two walls have windows; three walls have doorways—it was a challenge to set the room up for their needs. You can see that the buffet overlaps the drapery. Sometimes, you just have to make it work.

One of their favorite rooms in the house is the dining room. They have had my husband and me over for dinner many times, and it's always special. We did the room in the perfect shade of coral. Finding the silk wall covering in the right value was easier than finding the silk for the drapes to match. The cord on the chair is one of the fashion details I love. We banded the drapes in a beaded trim to add that touch of jewelry.

RIGHT: Also an addition, the library is the mirror architectural image of the new entry. Intricate and seamless, the shelves and moldings are all one composition. Again, the windows were so beautiful we left them uncovered. We brought in touches of the most delicate shade of coral in the rug and the two pillows. PAGE 72: The palette here is all about understated tones and textures. PAGE 73: The antique table continues the mix of old and new, dark and light.

You can sequence color strategically throughout a house, but it doesn't have to be obvious. The subtle reference to coral shows up in room after room in different guises—in the pattern of a curtain fabric, as pillows, in a bouquet, as cording. In the rooms that are mostly shades of bone and neutral, the coral color really stands out.

OPPOSITE: When we found this casual, handwoven rug for the family dining room, it was the perfect shade of coral. The painted brick fireplace reflects the style of the exterior of the house. The branch chandelier is a nod to the outdoors. PAGE 76: As in many of the houses we work on, the kitchen is central to everything. I love the juxtaposition of the classic kitchen with the iron-and-crystal chandelier and the button and cording details on the slipcovered barstools—it's just so pretty. PAGE 77: The mudroom at the back of the house connects the billiard room to a guesthouse, the gardens, and their garages. I love turning transitional spaces into rooms, especially when they're used every day. The slate floor, the wood doors painted to resemble iron, along with the built-in lockers work for this house.

LEFT: A simple, pretty palette of blue and platinum makes their master bedroom a serene, quiet retreat. PAGE 80: Their bar is a family heirloom. We loved it in a composition with the Regency mirror and the birds. PAGE 81: In the billiard room, we used many of their existing pieces, including the rug, pool table, and wing chairs. The owners had always wanted a dark blue room and this seemed the perfect spot since it's at the end of the house and connects to the gardens. We originally thought their rug wouldn't fit, but we got lucky. Then we added the red tape detail to the draperies to bring up that color from the floor.

St. James

PAGE 83: When the owner moved back to Columbia, South Carolina, from New Orleans after Hurricane Katrina, she brought many of her antiques with her. RIGHT: The minute you walk into this house, it's all about style. This entry is my ideal of sophisticated simplicity. Everything is painted a high-gloss white, with the front door accentuated in a lacquered Farrow & Ball black. The marble floor is a bold, Chanel-inspired riff on traditional entry hall patterns. For a note of sophisticated whimsy, we hung a Murano chandelier. Standing proudly against one wall is a nineteenth-century Italian walnut commode.

Design really does reflect life's twists and turns. After Hurricane Katrina, this client moved from New Orleans back to Columbia, South Carolina. She then met her husband, who had already purchased this property. Both are great lovers of architecture and design. She has a passion for details, so she was deeply involved in the design process. They commissioned architect Ruard Veltman to create the house, a grand interpretation of a traditional Charleston single house rendered in Greek Revival style. With its limestone and stucco facade, stone entry portico, and long side porches (or "piazzas") overlooking the formal gardens, it looks classic from the street, and as if it had always been there.

She is very chic, so of course she wanted her home to be the same. Because they entertain frequently, the spaces had to function well for that purpose. She had brought many antiques with her from New Orleans. They had also begun to collect contemporary art together. Our challenge was to make sure that the architectural envelope would enhance the beauty of their furnishings, art, and accessories. Fortunately, she loves the aesthetics of the Regency period. Strictly disciplined and graceful, it was the perfect design inspiration for combining and balancing the classic and the modern.

Because the rooms are primarily neutral with hints of platinum and gold, their favorite saturated hues—like the green velvet in the entry and the magenta velvet in

Four sets of black-painted doors punctuate the flow on the ground level. This pair opens onto a dining room done in champagne tones. The de Gournay wall covering at Bergdorf Goodman inspired her chinoiserie wall treatment. The antique table was hers. With chairs in linen velvet, corded in purple, and sisal on the floor, the room is effervescent, but in a muted, timeless way. Not shown are window coverings in an Osborne & Little silk taffeta with stripes of magenta, green, purple, and platinum. They inspired the bold color accents.

the living room—harmonize beautifully. Even when rooms are as visually connected to one another as theirs are, I find that different colors in different rooms will work as long as they are of the same value. It is so interesting to me how I am continually inspired by my clients. After the owner showed me these bold colors that she loved, I was in a showroom in San Francisco and happened upon a silk taffeta striped in magenta, green, purple, and platinum. This started the story of the house. I have to admit that the workroom was surprised and had many comments. But when the drapes were installed, they were fabulous.

ABOVE: With its classical details, their newly built house looks as if it's always been there. OPPOSITE: The John Soane mantel appeals to the owners' love of the Regency period. The amethyst, amber, and clear rock crystal dahlia sconces are so beautiful. They're the art pieces that anchor that wall. We layered in the Carolyn Carr painting, and played with the contrast of modern and antique. FOLLOWING SPREAD: In this particular house, I used color on much larger pieces than I would ordinarily. Making the final decision on the perfect shade of magenta for this sofa took a lot of looking at samples. I love the classic champagne detail that we added to the sofa. When it was finished, it was perfect in the room. PAGES 92–93: The living room is the core of the house, and reflects the clients' style. Its four sets of black lacquered doors are a strong architectural element and connect to the other spaces.

ABOVE AND OPPOSITE: Although we kept the kitchen tailored—a highly functional work space in white with weathered gray armoires—we did dress it up just a little more than usual to suit their lifestyle. The custom black hood over the range with the metallic detail makes a very subtle reference back to the black lacquered doors. I love the French pastry table found at 1stdibs in New York. And the Belgian chairs in rustic linen are so comfortable.

We based the aesthetic on New Orleans, French influences, and the antiques they already owned. The fluted molding in the hallway is one of the Regency-inspired architectural elements that make these spaces feel so richly detailed. This is a beautiful frame for peeking into the custom paneled library.

We made this hall much more contemporary in feeling by painting it to look like white plaster; the arched ceiling is painted in a metallic shade of oyster. On the fireplace wall, we created a composition with unusual ostrich egg sconces, a petite seventeenth-century mirror, a Hunt Slonem painting, and a sculptural metal light fixture. It's so captivating, you can't help but enter the room.

To give the library its warm glow, everything in the room is waxed a golden, honeyed shade. The deep purple accents in the throw and the desk chair provide a perfect complement to the honey tones. Other than the fireplace with its Greek key motif (echoing the trim on the living room's magenta sofa), the details here are more clean-lined and classically modern than in the rest of the house. The tiger velvet throw on the ottoman may look as if it's just draped casually over the top, but we had it made that way. And it fits perfectly.

RIGHT: Upstairs, the master bedroom also looks over the garden. With walls painted a soft platinum, silk drapes at the window, and a silk rug, the room has a shimmery feel in daylight and so much romance at night. The custom Louis XVI bed is in keeping with their love of French things. The Empire-period mirror introduces sparkle and age. The chairs are vintage modern. PAGE 102: The architect designed her vanity, which looks like a vintage piece of furniture. We lacquered it white and found the most stunning, overscale, vintage Baguès sconces and dressed the room in pink taffeta curtains. PAGE 103: To create a feeling of unity in the master suite, we kept the floor consistent throughout. I really love to bring design and details into a master bathroom. This is one of the house's most beautiful rooms. The large-scale photograph by Paul Lange also reflects the garden.

ABOVE: Here are nature's original versions of the foyer's saturated green and the master bath's luscious pink. The chairs are a 1930s sunburst design attributed to François Carré. OPPOSITE: The loggia resembles an old Charleston side porch with louvered shutters and an antique marble floor in a classical pattern. Although it is outside, we've furnished it as we would an interior world. The owners have their coffee there every morning.

Tuxedo

I n Atlanta, we really appreciate classical architecture. This young family of five also loves the traditional architectural aesthetic. That is why they purchased their neo-Georgian home in Buckhead, designed by Atlanta's Harrison Design. But they wanted their interiors to be much more edited and modern. To me, it was all about sophisticated simplicity.

They came to us without much existing furniture, and were prepared to do the house in its entirety. They also wanted to begin a collection of original artwork. We thought it would be a wonderful decorating project. Very soon, we discovered it would be much more. We decided to start with the foyer, where they made it clear that they wanted to change literally everything. Instead of ripping things out, we convinced them to paint all the interior architecture a high-gloss white. We switched out the existing railing on the floating stair with one handcrafted in iron and bronze by Charles Calhoun, one of our great local artisans. We designed an overscale glass light fixture, which we had made in England, and hung it from the dome. Then we regrouted, honed, and buffed the floor. Just these few gestures transformed the feeling of the house completely.

PAGE 107: Because the entry is so expansive, we were able to create a composition of sculptural elements of steel, glass, brass, and iron. We added some glamour with the Steven Seinberg paintings. OPPOSITE: Whenever you do a sculptural floating stair, its underneath space becomes a challenge. Dressed in linen with a velvet cushion, the Saladino bench we placed there almost looks like limestone.

This house already had a certain elegance, with beautiful crown moldings, a limestone fireplace, and more. I have learned that using shades of white throughout immediately brings any interior to a more modern place, one that really shows off everything you layer into it, from furnishings and fabrics to objects and art. To give their home a collected feel with a more modern sensibility, we emphasized comfort, mixed the up-to-date with the classic, and edited closely and carefully. It is the juxtapositions of these elements that give these rooms their personality.

ABOVE: To me, classical architecture feels as if it's always been there. OPPOSITE: These clients didn't want much color, so we introduced it in ways that weren't overbearing, like the trio of oil paintings over the sofa by Katharina Chapuis. We'll often arrange the furnishings around the fireplace, but the proportions here led us to push the furniture to the wall. And that plan led us to the very large sofa by Christian Liaigre. At 108 inches long, its scale is unusual in a residential space. Its modern look within this kind of classically inspired architecture is also unexpected.

When the doors and windows were their original dark mahogany, they felt like a block against the view. Painting them white was a big step that changed this space even more dramatically than we expected. Inspired by French modern, the coffee table is scaled for today's living. Other pieces in the room continue the brass and glass look, with the chair's gold leafing as an accent. With everything in the room so light and clear, the one piece that stands out is the piano.

PAGE 114: Instead of ripping out the library, we ebonized the faded paneling with a stain and did everything else in cream. PAGE 115: With its fabulous art—including an Anke Schofield painting over the fireplace—very modern French light fixture, and their own antique books and objects, this room was probably the biggest surprise for them in terms of design's powers of transformation. RIGHT: When a dining room is full of art, it can take the focus off the people around the table. That's why I love the custom Gracie wall covering in silver and bone here: it makes an artistic statement, but quietly. In the mix of classic and modern, the rock crystal lamps are more traditional in their forms, while the rock crystal chandelier is totally today. The Hermès dishes, silverware, crystal, and napkins bring in so much detail and sparkle. With its gorgeous glass pieces, the massive mirror looks almost like a work of art. PAGE 118: Even when you're doing an edited house, the details are what bring the house together. A jeweled bead on the drapery trim adds a subtle feeling of couture to the tailored curtain panels. PAGE 119: It was so special showing the owners how a classic wall covering could play into a modern vision.

When you do
a house in neutrals
and whites, one
of the prettiest ways
to make the rooms
come alive is to play
texture off texture.

The breakfast room may be my favorite spot in the house.
We built in the banquette as a classic window seat with leather
cushions that wipe down easily. It's so cozy, and comfortably
seats six. Most important, it adds an architectural element
that defines this fabulous corner window. Tailored and almost
not there, the woven shades diffuse the light beautifully.

The kitchen, breakfast room, and family room are basically one space. The challenge for us was to make sure they relate to one another visually, yet still have their own identities. The family room is quiet, comfortable, and casual. Because it's tone on tone and all in neutrals, it inspires the family to continue to add personal items over time. The doors and windows were originally stained dark here as well. We debated for a long time whether or not to leave them that way, but once we had painted the other doors in the house, we realized we also had to paint these. Right away, the room became more connected to the outdoors and more architectural in its feel.

The master bedroom was so large we decided to upholster the walls in linen to create a feeling of warmth and embrace. Our greatest challenge here was the color because silk and silk velvet reflect the light differently than linen, lacquer, and silver leaf. We always appreciate the simplicity of a tailored bed, but we also love to layer it. A trim detail gives the edge of the drapes such a beautiful finish.

ABOVE: When we work on family houses, the children's rooms are always a focus. We want to make them fun, special, and a favorite place. For the boy's room, we did everything in gray and natural linen, with one accent wall in orange. OPPOSITE: The daughter's room is a lovely shade of lavender, with painted ceiling coffers that pick up the hue in the headboard and the detail in the unique drapery fabric.

COUNTRY

So much of creating a house with a sense of place has to do with finding ways to connect the inside and the outside. I love using design to express that relationship, especially in a country house where people want to live in both places, and to focus on nature. When the interior architecture references the exterior, and when the inside flows effortlessly to the outdoors, a country house just feels right.

Port Clyde

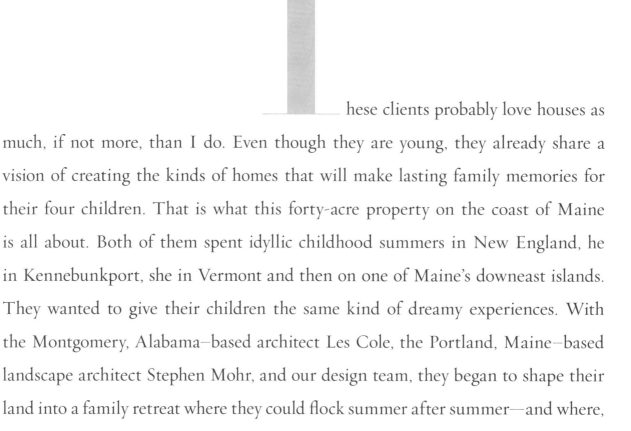

These clients probably love houses as much, if not more, than I do. Even though they are young, they already share a vision of creating the kinds of homes that will make lasting family memories for their four children. That is what this forty-acre property on the coast of Maine is all about. Both of them spent idyllic childhood summers in New England, he in Kennebunkport, she in Vermont and then on one of Maine's downeast islands. They wanted to give their children the same kind of dreamy experiences. With the Montgomery, Alabama–based architect Les Cole, the Portland, Maine–based landscape architect Stephen Mohr, and our design team, they began to shape their land into a family retreat where they could flock summer after summer—and where, eventually, their children would do the same with the next generation. It was so interesting to me that the first building they designed was the pool house. They understood that by creating this gathering place for family and friends, they were defining the spirit of the property and how it would eventually unfold.

PAGES 130–131: Inside and out, the pool house set the stage for everything to come. PRECEDING SPREAD: The pool house is architecturally stunning and unique, but it is classic in terms of what you picture when you think of Maine. OPPOSITE: We decided to go with blue and white in the most traditional sense—that is, using only one print. An iconic antique eagle presides over the room, a perfect piece of Americana and just right for this property. Oversize Belgian sofas and chairs in rustic linen give the room a fresh, young spirit. With a mix of really fine antiques and art, it becomes a space meant for making memories.

ABOVE: With a pool table, this room in the pool house becomes the family game room and hangout.
OPPOSITE: Our client is an amazing cook, and uses her kitchens all the time. What's really fun about this one is that because it's not in the main house, we were able do something a bit different. And so we did.

ABOVE: In the pool house bathroom, a custom wall covering and antiqued mirror establish a classic mood, while an open sink and a tile floor layer in more modern but still timeless elements. OPPOSITE: In the pool house's sole bedroom, we kept the blue-and-white theme, but varied the tones, patterns, and textures to create a room with an enduring look.

In both the pool house and the main house, we've included the high, the low, the casual, the dressy, the contemporary, and the antique. It's what I love about style—and their style—that we can bring in such a mix of things in a way that makes the special pieces feel even more special.

When they first bought the property, they decided to take their time to figure out what they wanted to do with it. After freshening up a small, existing cottage, they moved in and began planning construction that would lie lightly on the land. First came the pool and pool house. A few years later, they began work on the family house. These additions show their love of art, design, and decorating, as well as of antiques and artwork. What has been so fascinating for me about working on this project with them was seeing their understanding of how a foundation of tradition in design translates into a foundation for lasting family traditions.

We painted the outside of the front door of the main house in blue and banded the sisal rug to match. All the rooms and hallways of the house are so architecturally interesting. To really show off the details—the coffered ceilings, wall moldings, and baseboards—we painted the entire architectural envelope in a shade of white.

In the main house, we wanted to incorporate many antiques, as well as art and wonderful pieces of blue-and-white porcelain, some inherited, others collected. To design and create a house that feels young, we edited very carefully to make sure that the rooms were comfortable, airy, and full of beautiful things, but not overdecorated.

In the living room, we decided to include a bold geometric rug. This one is very fun and whimsical, but classic, and sets a whole different atmosphere in the room. I think the mix of blue-and-white patterns—a custom-colored floral print, tie-dye, geometric, and stripe—is unexpected and a bit unconventional. Yet it works because of the neutral sofas and chairs, plus the solids and accent pieces in the same shades of blue.

In the dining area across from the living room, we created custom banquette seating that backs up to the pass-through wall from the Christopher Peacock kitchen. She had the table made by Jeff Soderbergh, an artisan based in Newport, Rhode Island, who's known for crafting sustainable furnishings. I love the juxtaposition of white with the cabinetry's stained wood.

This house was perfect for
a fitted galley kitchen. We kept
things simple and functional,
so the surfaces are white and
walnut, with antique rugs to
infuse a bit of color and pattern.
Adjacent, there's a little bar that
opens through into this space.

It's so interesting that instead of curtains, we did a custom brass pot rack to hang
in front of the window, which we flanked with brass sconces. We did all of the kitchen
knobs, faucets, and hardware in brass, because it felt so classic Maine.

The main stair hall sets the design concept for the entire house, so what it includes is key. Painting the architectural envelope all white enhances the space and the details. The dark wood and sisal establish a tone of casual elegance.

As simple as we kept these interiors, we used beautiful antiques, artwork, and accessories to suggest the element of time.

ABOVE AND OPPOSITE: This beautiful oak-paneled library gives the house a sense of history. All of our clients are finding that they can spend much more time at their vacation homes if they have a real place to work. We designed this very large room to serve that purpose. It also functions as a TV room and place to play board games and cards.

The library is at the end of one hall. It's cozy and comfortable, with sisal rugs and art and antiques from the family's collection. We also included some modern elements, such as the end tables, with vintage lamps and classic contemporary upholstered pieces.

We paid close attention to design and detail, wanting to create spaces that are classic, young, and meant to last. Instead of the traditional blue, white, and red, the boys' room is blue, white, and orange. The geometric wall covering, striped rug, and vintage flags give it a very graphic and fun look, but one that's still anchored in tradition by antique chests and twin beds.

PAGE 156: The master bath includes a custom-made mosaic tile floor. PAGE 157: Bright and full of light, the master bedroom has a completely different aesthetic from the rest of the house. OPPOSITE: The boys' room opens to another sleeping room so that all the boys and their cousins can hang out together. The custom striped rug and vintage naval flags add a nautical note. Even here, we wanted furnishings that would last, so we had the beds brought from London. The English chest of drawers is a family heirloom that dates to 1870.

OPPOSITE: The enclosed porch is attached to the main house. Linen curtains give the exterior room the feeling of an interior room. ABOVE: The placement of the swimming pool creates a stunning connection to the ocean.

The chickens have a wonderful home in the coop, while the barn houses many of the family's other animals: a menagerie of alpacas, fainting goats, and a pig. They've also put in an orchard, and vegetable and flower gardens.

Palmetto Bluff

P eople with second homes usually want them to offer scenarios for living that provide a real escape from their day-to-day lifestyle. So I take a very specific approach to editing, as the story of this vacation house in Palmetto Bluff, near Hilton Head, South Carolina, shows. Pursley Dixon Architects, the Charlotte-based firm, designed it as a riff on the vernacular of Low Country living. They also made it very chic. All the downstairs areas connect to a two-story living/ family room at the core. Relating our work to these references, we kept the interiors casual, with a light, tone-on-tone palette, lots of texture, comfortable contemporary furnishings, sisal, and indoor/outdoor fabrics throughout. Then we added in a few antiques, found objects, and modern art to give each room a distinctive edge.

Many of us today expect our rooms to serve more than one purpose and to dress up and dress down almost at will. In a vacation house like this one, that is especially true. Here, from the moment you walk in the front door, this concept is at play because when you see the large table, you immediately ask yourself: "Is this a dining room, or is this an entry?"

PAGE 164: The "chandelier" over the entry hall/dining table gives a hint of the darkened steel elements to come. To create this light fixture, we took six individual elements and hung them in a random pattern. OPPOSITE: This low-ceilinged foyer can also function for dining. For everyday, we style the table with a few, easily movable accessories. For a meal, we'll set it properly, pull in chairs from the other rooms, and push the bench against the wall.

Porches that run the length of the house are key to the Low Country architectural vernacular. The architects ran them around the entire house, and stepped them down below the window line so that they would not obstruct the views from the interior.

Obviously, I think the vacation lifestyle is not about overdecorating. It is actually not about decorating at all. What really matters is creating comfort in every part of the living space, inside and out. At the same time, if the spaces don't have style, being on vacation there won't be much fun.

ABOVE: Broad porches are typical of the Low Country vernacular. OPPOSITE: Here you can see just how much more edited and minimal a second home can be. It's all about textures and layering. This main room is two stories high, making it feel especially airy for a vacation home. We positioned two main seating groups for maximum comfort and use. One centers on a pair of banquette sofas nested into a bay of windows; the other focuses on the steel-framed fireplace wall, which also houses the TV.

PRECEDING SPREAD: In keeping with the location and vernacular, the furnishings and accessories have a rustic elegance. ABOVE: Signed, Danish modern chairs by Kaare Klint from the Paris Flea Market introduce a European style that speaks to the steel storage wall. OPPOSITE: A metal mesh curtain screens the fireplace. The contrasting metals gave us visual cues. A whisper of blue gray here refers to the water outside.

The kitchen is modern and tailored, with a sleek central island, open shelves above the counters, and gray-painted contemporary cabinets below. It flows into the main, two-story room, and also to a fabulous pantry where we continued the open shelves. All of the lower cabinets are stock cabinetry. Painting them gave them a special, custom look. We used the open shelving because of the window placement, and allowed the dishes and glassware to become part of the overall composition.

The back entry is in keeping with the Low Country fashion. We found this rustic, antique table just after we had joined the team. It was our first purchase, and ended up defining the aesthetic throughout the house. It's so overscale that when we brought it to the location, we were just hoping it would fit. Wherever we are, we look for things that will be special to a project. These kinds of unusual pieces create timeless style.

ABOVE: We often run the wood floors from the bedrooms into the baths, especially in houses where the two spaces are closely connected. The opaque glass walls reflect the blue-gray-green sea glass tiles in the master bath. OPPOSITE: We did all the bedrooms in a style that's comfortable and tailored, with ready-made bedding, sisal flooring, and a few well-placed details.

OPPOSITE: The patterns in this bedroom pick up on the palmettos outside and the stripes that we've used throughout. ABOVE: In a second home, you always end up needing more beds. We used this odd space under the roof to put in these two facing daybeds. The Missoni blankets bring in the kind of chic details that we love. PAGE 182: For flexible family dining on the porch, we installed two of my tables from Ballard Designs, which fit neatly together either side by side to form a square or end to end to create a long table. PAGE 183: Docks are iconic in the Low Country, and the ultimate places to sit, have a drink, and watch the sun rise and set.

Canterbury

There is such a thing as love at first sight with houses. This young family of four know the feeling well. They experienced it the first time they saw Canterbury, as this historic, neo-Georgian house in Richmond, Virginia, is called. Designed by William Lawrence Bottomley (1883–1951) in the 1920s or '30s, it sits, like a country estate, on ten acres in the city's heart. But as it was it did not meet the family's needs. They wanted their home to be classic, but young and interesting rather than traditional-traditional.

They addressed first things first, putting together the design team so we could all collaborate from the start. Madison Spencer Architects from Charlottesville helped reinvent the house and designed an addition to respect what already existed. Charlottesville-based landscape architects Rieley and Associates created its sweeping gardens. I weighed in on spatial matters as well as decorating.

As we took the house down to the studs, many interesting issues came up. One involved the circular stair at the house's core. In its original form, the stair was too small for today's lifestyle. To expand it enough for family use—and so that it would recreate the look of the original and fit seamlessly—we had to redefine the entry foyer.

PAGE 185: This neo-Georgian house by William Lawrence Bottomley dates to the early 1920s or '30s. OPPOSITE: To showcase the renewed entry architecture, we painted everything in linen white. In pink silk velvet, the petite Gustavian chair adds a pinpoint focus. FOLLOWING SPREAD: We turned this half of the large formal dining room into a gallery-like space, accenting the door, with its view of the James River. The exquisite mirrored doorways house the family's crystal and china. The pediment is original to the house.

These clients love antiques and gorgeous fabrics. They also have a growing collection of traditional oil paintings. And dogs. But they did not care to live in a museum, or in spaces weighed down by too much decoration. So once we remastered the spaces and their flow, we were able to select palettes, fabrics, furnishings, and accessories that were classic enough to make sense with the architecture, but young and spirited enough to complement the family. They wanted every room in the house to be used—no matter how formal or fancy. And that's what we've created.

OPPOSITE: The gilt finishes bring so much glamour to the formal living room, and feel completely fresh against the linen white walls. ABOVE: Though this neo-Georgian house is in a historic Richmond neighborhood in the city's center, its entry suggests a country estate. FOLLOWING SPREAD: With its silks, velvets, and antiques, this room truly reflects the family's aesthetic; their daughter always practices on the grand piano.

The dining
room walls
are lacquered
a lustrous,
French-
inspired
shade of blue.
It's so chic—
and so iconic.

We've arranged the dining room
to be as flexible as possible. They
can host intimate dinners. And
by turning the table around and
inserting a few leaves, they can seat
at least twenty comfortably.

194

ABOVE: This custom-colored, hand-painted silk wall covering from de Gournay repeats the blue-gray tones that echo throughout the house. That touch of pink beaded trim on the drapery picks up the pink flowers in the wall covering. OPPOSITE: It's interesting that the front door, which we lacquered in black, is so petite, yet so strong. With the classic black-and-white patterned floor, it creates a smart transition zone between the outside and the indoors.

What I really love is a house that's Continental. So in this English house, we've used English pieces, of course, along with pieces from France, Italy, and elsewhere in Europe. The result is rooms that are sophisticated and traditional in spirit, but not literal.

The original kitchen was out of another era—one with cooks and servants. We expanded it substantially to open it up and update it for the young family and their lifestyle. The Calacatta Viola marble behind the stove, wide-plank floors, and the hammered metal lanterns over the island tether it back to a memory of its former self.

We took a more traditionally
English approach in the library. The
creamy/taupe-y palette provides a
wonderful stage for their red-and-
blue Oriental carpet, horse sculpture,
pheasant, and the oil painting of
English spaniels over the classic, neo-
Georgian mantel. These references
seemed absolutely right in this more
casual, cozy room, and so appropriate
to Richmond's English heritage.

One of the challenges in a historic house has to do with proportions. Your tendency is always to scale pieces down because the rooms are smaller than today's and the ceilings are usually lower. But by building up the scale, and even sometimes going overscale, you can bring great energy to a room that would otherwise look too traditional.

In the master bedroom, our challenge was to find a way to use a documentary fabric that felt stylish and timeless for the twenty-first century. Surrounding it with luxurious textures in a neutral palette gives it a lightness of being. The contrasting eras of the bedside tables contribute to the play on tradition. Touches of gilt and blue velvet add layers of depth and liveliness and pull in references from the exquisite documentary fabric.

ABOVE: We brought more English-inspired references into the husband's dressing room, wrapping it in his family's tartan and adding the antique writing desk. With all the dark wood tones and blues, the light rug on the floor makes the room feel more contemporary. OPPOSITE: For the son, we carved out a private domain from an attic space on the third floor, repeating the tartan element with a classic Black Watch plaid. His bed fits under the slope of the roof like a ship's cabin, and has extra storage underneath.

The indoor/outdoor component is always a part of working on a house, but it has become a larger focus for my clients now. They appreciate thinking through what makes a sense of place and how we can use design to create it.

In the crispness of this all-white loggia, the brickwork of the Palladian arch stands out. I love it when the architectural elements offer graphic impact that enhances our design.

SHORE

One of my favorite kinds of houses is a beach house, because I love being by the ocean. Most of them today have open floor plans and large spaces inside and out where families and friends can hang out together. For me, though, the real beauty of a beach house is about the details, textures, and beach tones, with references to the sea and the sky.

Sea Island

Sea Island is a classic, Southern destination, and it continues to attract people who, like this family, want to build beautiful oceanfront homes. Architect Thomas Thaddeus Truett, who is based in Saint Simons Island, Georgia, designed their Mediterranean Revival–style house in the spirit of Sea Island's original cottages from the late 1920s and early '30s. He says its details show the influence of that era's great architects, among them Addison Mizner and Francis Abreu. Alex Smith Garden Design was also part of our team.

Our challenge was to give this new house the kind of patina that makes it feel like it has history. The key to accomplishing this was using pieces of furniture and objects that relate to the scale of the architecture, which is quite grand. Even so, I saw no need to overdo things. We selected designs that reflected some of the house's unique architectural details—the deep plaster walls, decorative windows, and railings—and made subtle references to them. Wherever the eye turned, we wanted it to find exquisite design details.

Happily, the more this kind of house is lived in, the more beautiful it becomes. This family of five entertains all the time, so the house has been full of life from day one.

PAGE 210: The depth of these plaster walls harks back to an earlier era. OPPOSITE: It is so important to me that the interior design reflects the architecture. All of the pieces we brought in to this entry foyer make up a composition that responds to the symmetry of the space. PAGE 214: The stairwell's unique forms, materials, and scale inspired our choice of lighting fixtures. PAGE 215: When we're installing a house, we're always surprised by how each piece finds its best place. We intended the Italian antique table to anchor the stair hall. But when we placed it under the floating stair, it made the perfect arrangement.

From the beginning, we worked with the architect not only on the interior plan but also on all the finishes, from the dark iron railings to the teak detailing to the stone flooring that travels from the inside rooms to those immediately outside the walls. One main focus was the decorative tile work. We traveled to Los Angeles, which, with its indoor/outdoor lifestyle, showcases many tile and stone details and options. The trip was completely inspiring, and we ended up using tile throughout to enhance the home's Mediterranean flavor. The clients loved the result so much that they now spend almost six months of the year here.

ABOVE: The architect wanted this house to capture the spirit of Sea Island's original cottages.
OPPOSITE: Inside and out, the house is meant to look aged to give it a sense of permanence. On our trip to Los Angeles, we found antique mantels and custom rugs as well as tile. The period French mantel layers in the patina of time we were looking for. The story of its discovery has become part of the story of this house. I love the juxtaposition of the stunning waxed painting by Dusty Griffith.

Even though this house is right on the water—and we've used lots of gorgeous watery blue hues throughout—it's not your typical beach house. We wanted it to feel like a much older place, the kind where you can see the layers of its past lives in the present. To create that sensibility, we mixed antiques with classic upholstery pieces and natural fabrics. This gives the rooms a dressed-up element that's casual at the same time. The living room's custom Oushak, so muted, pulls everything together.

What's important about this kind of house is that it's designed for casual living, so it has a modern, open floor plan. Within this one large space, the living room flows into the dining room and, finally, to the kitchen.

The decorative tile work belongs to the Mediterranean style of the architecture. We thought if we used tile in this way, it would help the house look and feel as if it had been there for a long, long time. Since we don't see much Mediterranean influence or this kind of detail in the South, for inspiration we went to Los Angeles, where this use of tile is both historic and common.

We were able to design this little window seat and bench in the kitchen to create a breakfast nook. There's a larger table in the middle of the space, but this is perfect for times when the owners just want to sit and read the paper with a cup of coffee.

This house is all about family and friends, so we gave them a very large kitchen. Behind it is a pantry kitchen that houses double ovens, other appliances, and storage. One of the wonderful aspects of this arrangement is that when they clear the table, they have a place to put the dishes that is completely out of sight. The lifestyle here is indoor/outdoor, so all the doors along the one wall open out to a furnished loggia. At the windows, we did very simple, unlined linen drapes, dressed up with a beautiful banding.

 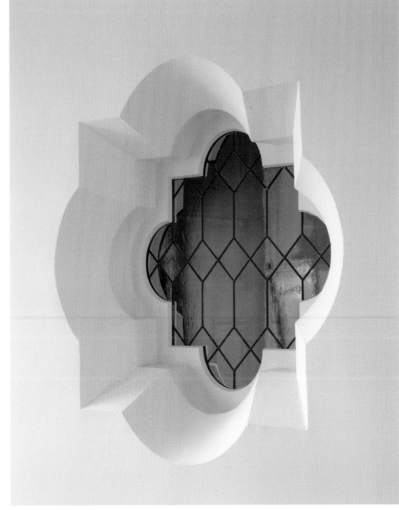

OPPOSITE: Even the back stairs from the dining area reflect the touch of tile. ABOVE, LEFT: We found these vases in the perfect shades of aqua, and they look just like sea glass. ABOVE, RIGHT: The foundation of the house incorporates these deep plaster walls. In several places, the architect did these unusual windows that become sculptural elements. PAGE 228: The dark-stained, classic Italian wood pieces really contribute to the Mediterranean feel. PAGE 229: We left the pecky cypress ceilings in their natural state, just finishing them with wax and oil. For a special touch, the dining room chairs are topped with carved seashells.

ABOVE: The mudroom is on the way to the loggia. We covered its back wall in a glass mosaic and outfitted it with refrigerated drawers and a sink so the family can use it as a bar. OPPOSITE: In the powder room, a striking, custom-colored mosaic tile wall shows off the antique mirrors, sconces, and a stone vessel sink. I love the surprise of a beautifully designed powder room. PAGE 232: The owner wanted a real library where he could work and also relax, read, and watch TV. This room has the most spectacular view. PAGE 233: Pecky cypress paneling covers the library walls and ceiling, and is reminiscent of the original bar at the Cloister, Sea Island's legendary grand hotel.

We wanted the master bedroom upstairs to be subtle, soothing, and quiet. The printed curtain fabric gave us a start for the palette of blues. The rug is mostly cream with platinum. I love the simplicity of an upholstered headboard and matching dust skirt with just a layer of white linen—and then a channeled velvet throw. Beds can be challenging because they're so large, but here the beamed ceiling, iron windows, and views give the eye something compelling to see in every direction.

ABOVE: In the master bedroom, the palette of materials and colors is simple but handsome—and also quite luxurious. OPPOSITE: Embroidered bedding is a small touch of beauty that makes a big difference.

The family has three daughters, and we designed their bedrooms to reflect their unique personalities. The scale of this one is large enough for a pair of queen-size iron beds. There's something so classic and timeless about the Oushak rug here. I think you could come back to this room in twenty years and maybe you would just have to redo the bedding.

ABOVE: To me, design is so much about architecture. OPPOSITE: When you look at Mediterranean architecture, it is all about the tile, so we continued our focus on decorative tile throughout all the bathrooms. Each is unique and very special. And as it turned out, the clients loved this.

ABOVE: In the youngest daughter's bedroom, we went with a bright coral print that looks like an ikat and used a solid coral for the headboard, dust skirt, and piping on the sofa. I'm always inspired at the beach by the corals as well as the blues and all the muted colors. OPPOSITE: A touch of whimsy and fun mixed with the classics brings personality to the room.

ABOVE: This bath started with the tile, which inspired its casual, more bohemian look. It goes with the nearby bunk room. OPPOSITE: The bunks gave us a chance to do something stronger in this game/TV room, designed for sleeping and hanging out with family and friends. The built-in sofa wraps around the room and has drawers underneath for extra storage.

This loggia runs the length of the house from the living room to the kitchen, with access from every area and stone floors that transition from inside to outside. We've arranged and furnished it in a mirror image of the interior in terms of function, but with materials that are perfect for the exterior. The client wanted color here, so we brought out the blue and white in a bolder version to stand up to the brilliant sun.

Naples

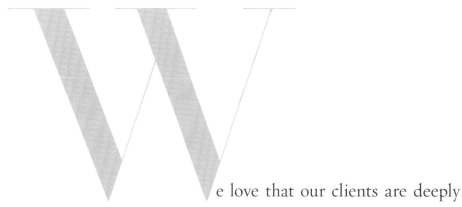

e love that our clients are deeply involved in the homes we create for them, every step of the way. With these clients, it is even more than that. They are longtime family friends. This house in Naples, Florida, is the third we have done with them. By now we know them and their tastes and needs very well, but this house is a bit of a departure in several ways. They are American traditionalists, and passionate collectors of everything from paintings and American antiques to Americana. They love color and pattern, and lots of it. And she prefers a more decorated home. But for this house, they both wanted something more edited, crisp, and modern. I told them they should do it all in white.

They had purchased a bungalow of sorts in one of the city's older neighborhoods, because for this home they wanted a small footprint. They brought on Herscoe Hajjar Architects of Naples to help make it more modern. Part of the team from the beginning, we worked with them to simplify and open up the interior architecture and make sure that the floor plan flowed effortlessly from the front door to the back porch and pool area.

PAGE 249: We suggested a floor of white stone embedded with seashells that goes from the entry all the way through the house and out to the pool. Venetian plaster on the walls adds elegance and refinement, especially in juxtaposition with the stone and shell floor. OPPOSITE: In this luminous entry, we introduced accents of pink in the chic stripe on the chairs. The notes of pink begin at the entry, and reappear throughout the rest of the house.

The architects gave the exterior a classic, contemporary facade, but I think it is still reminiscent of the former bungalow. Inside, we kept the architectural envelope fairly understated. In terms of the all-white palette, I did not entirely get my way. She loves pink, so of course we mixed in the most gorgeous shade of peony and some calming, watery blues here and there. The materials and fabrics are on the elegant side, and so are some of the accents, yet we have put the emphasis on comfort, just like always. The result is a somewhat different look for them, but it is in keeping with its surroundings and with what they love—and with what we do, too.

ABOVE: The architects transformed the existing bungalow into a more contemporary residence. I think the house looks so pretty and modern now. OPPOSITE: The renovated exterior inspired our choices for the clean and edited look of the interior.

The architecture is understated and airy, and yet it has plenty of interest, too. In their almost all-white living room, their growing collection of contemporary art has a perfect backdrop. Little spots of pink and blue stand out. So do the more modern elements, like the sculptural iron ceiling fixture, as well as the more traditional elements, like the candelabra sconces. The wool and silk rug gives the room a lovely, shimmery softness underfoot.

When I talk about the strategic use of color, I think so much about this house. It's really all about white. But mixing in the pink and blue makes it interesting. And because there's really not much of either color, when they do appear, they feel striking.

A weathered buffet adds another layer of faded, sea-washed blue. With a limestone base and a fabulous driftwood top, the dining table is just so gorgeous. I love to mix the styles of the chairs, but they all need to be comfortable. Our signature, subtle details—the band at the hem of the chair and the Greek key trim on the curtains—continue the thread of pink that weaves its way through the house.

Sometimes I'll make a reference in one room to a color that you see in another. Often it's very subtle, but it helps to create a visual sequence that builds on itself. People don't always notice it. But it does give a house a great sensibility.

This kitchen is really simple, so details like a touch of tape with nailheads on the barstools stand out that much more. We used the same statuary white stone for both the island and the wall behind the range. On the island, it's in slab form; on the wall, in tiles.

OPPOSITE: The powder room is the perfect place for a more dressed-up look. All white and platinum, it adds a touch of fantasy and reflection. ABOVE: We carved out a small space for a bar, and lacquered it the most gorgeous shade of peony pink. The space opens into the main entry, and I love how it makes the hall a destination and ties it to the main room.

What's unique about this house is that it is a renovation. We worked with the architects and the clients on the plan to make sure the house was going to live the way they wanted it to and to keep the spaces architecturally simple.

The indoor/outdoor component of this house is one of its defining features, as family members spend as much time outdoors as they do inside. The home has an open floor plan, and it flows from the front door to the back porch, which can become an interior room when it is enclosed by a wall of screens that operates on remote control.

The family room is right off the kitchen. I know it looks blue because of the pillows, paintings, throw, and some shells, but really it's an all-white room— with a few, well-placed splashes of blue.

264

In the master bedroom, the palest of
blues whispers in all the whiteness.
The silver-leafed details add touches
of glamour and reflection.

ABOVE: Sometimes you want a room to feel like it's floating. Clear materials like glass and acrylic help create that illusion. OPPOSITE: The master bedroom is really spacious, allowing us to include this sitting area, which they use all the time.

ABOVE AND OPPOSITE: In the back of the house behind the kitchen is a wing with two guest bedrooms. In one, we put twin beds. In the other, we put a queen. The China Seas fabric we used is one of our clients' favorite patterns. One room has it in the coral colorway; the other, in the turquoise. They continue our color story, but in more saturated shades. FOLLOWING SPREAD: You can see how open the interior is, and just how organically the inside and outside spaces merge into one another.

Watercolor

When I am designing a beach house, I think about casual, comfortable spaces arranged so that everyone can hang out together, with a seamless indoor/outdoor flow. I want the rooms to be light, white, and bright, yet full of texture, tone, and detail. The furnishings need to be durable enough for wet bathing suits and sand. There should also be a few clear, visual reference points to tie the interiors to their surroundings. That is why I used gray driftwood tones, sand-colored woods, whitewashed furnishings, and white fabrics—plus a few turquoise accents that mirror the gorgeous blue-green color of the Gulf—in the renovation of this three-story beach house on Florida's Emerald Coast.

These clients, based in Nashville, have grown children and many grandchildren, so they wanted a family-friendly place with flexible, adaptable rooms. The multipurpose aesthetic starts at the entry, where a large table acts as a divider between the living space and the kitchen. It can obviously be set for meals. But it is also an invitation to spread out and read the paper, play cards or board games, or just stash the day's collection of seashells when they come in from the beach.

PAGE 274: At the beach, I like to edit the accessories so my clients can change them easily.
OPPOSITE: The table acts as a dividing line between the living area and kitchen. Accent pieces like the linen beach throw from Hermès in Paris add texture and splashes of color.

LEFT: The house is white, inside and out. OPPOSITE: Here, at the beach, a look that's almost undone feels just right. We love accessories that look great but that we don't need to worry about, like white pots in different shapes and sizes. These add texture and interest, whether they're empty or holding flowers or sprays of leaves. The Carolyn Carr painting that leans casually adds an abstract, contemporary touch and inserts another note of brilliant turquoise.

In the spirit of the beach, we did all the interior surfaces—floors, tables, beams, even wicker baskets—in shades of gray driftwood and sand. For the same reason, all the furniture is whitewashed. I always want enough beautiful objects to anchor each space. But I believe they should reflect a sense of place. Bits of coral or driftwood, rocks found on the beach, sea glass—even a modern piece—can add so much character. And even in this type of more edited, breezy interior, the dressmaker details we love make all the difference.

RIGHT: For the main room, all the design elements relate immediately back to the beach in color, texture, and form. A seating area with a pair of swivel chairs and an overscale sectional sofa encourages family members of all ages to spend time together here. Unlined linen drapes hang at the windows. When they're open, the views captivate. When they're closed, they diffuse the light. PAGE 282: The modern elements—lamps, art, trestle table, sisal rugs—help give this room its ease of look and touch. PAGE 283: The blue-and-white palette creates a timeless, classic feel and allows the clients to change the room's focus and look with different accessories as time goes on. If you remove these few blue notes, the room goes back to being all white— it's the people in the space, the family, who bring in the color.

I always say design is about the details. Even when we're taking a more edited approach, we want to find subtle ways to bring in unique touches and make them timeless. As for the details that we're known for, they may not get noticed immediately, but they add depth and dimension to the fabric of our projects.

A bay around a kitchen corner houses the family dining area. We centered it on a rustic round table and comfortable, slipcovered chairs with just a touch of blue and a little buttoned trim for character. The curved bench and a handmade rug from Afghanistan are also in understated tones that tie the room to the outdoors.

RIGHT: The kitchen opens off the main room. I love the jewelry element of design, so I often bring in different metal finishes. And I don't care if they match. Here the hammered metal elements add sparkle against the rustic, pecky cypress ceiling. PAGE 288: The beach scape inspired every choice we made for the interiors. PAGE 289: The tile on the powder room walls is spectacular, and it ties into the subtle color palette we used in the rest of the house. Because of the room's petite dimensions, we tucked the sink into the side of the space. Towels monogrammed with the number of the street address introduce another understated but special detail.

ABOVE: In general, the more extra bedrooms a beach house has, the better. In this house, the bedrooms range off the second- and third-floor landings. The sisal stair runner adds texture. OPPOSITE: The third floor has a bunk room for the grandchildren and their friends. We installed barn doors of pecky cypress so they can close it off from the playroom/TV room/ sitting room. PAGE 292: In this second-floor guest bedroom, we took a favorite, fun pattern and used it for the drapes, the headboard, and the dust skirt. PAGE 293: Like the rest of the house, the bathrooms are simple, modern, and bright.

In beach houses like this one, we have to plan the bedrooms to work for many different visiting family members and friends. So we don't design them to suit specific individuals, but we make sure each has its own look. The important thing is that they're comfortable for all and that they fit the style of the rest of the house. What's fun for us is that the family members who visit all pick their favorite room.

OPPOSITE: The second floor holds another set of bunk beds for the granddaughters. We made these just a bit more feminine, and included a drape to close them off from the hall. ABOVE: From the tile to the Moroccan benches, the adjoining bathroom is all in driftwood tones. PAGE 298: On the upstairs landings we continued the all-white palette with just a little touch of color from the painting and gray driftwood baskets. PAGE 299: Yes, we're at the beach. But the pool and poolside are very important living spaces, so we wanted them to relate to the interiors.

Because this pool is really an outdoor living room, we wanted to make it just as comfortable and adaptable as the one indoors, so we took a similar approach to choosing and arranging the furnishings. This large rattan sectional—it's capacious enough to fit the entire family, children and adults—makes an architectural statement when it's all in one. Yet it also comes apart easily to create different groupings. The little tables nearby are handy for drinks and things, and also can serve as extra seating options when there's an overflow crowd. The Hermès linen throw also ties back to the interior.

ACKNOWLEDGMENTS

A special thank you to Keith Arnold, my amazing associate and the vice president of our office. I am so grateful for your positive energy, unwavering enthusiasm and support for everything we do, and for making all that we create so memorable and fun. When work is fun, it is the best!

I also want to thank my incredible team and office who make Suzanne Kasler Interiors the best place to come to work every day: Keith Arnold, Julie Bowen, Karen Orr, Wright McCurdy, Carson Paschal, Kate Lloyd, Morgan Fields, Catherine Orr, and Paige Hamlin. Without all of you, I could not have achieved all we do, and what an exciting time we have together.

A special thank you to Carson Paschal, my marketing director, who has turned my ideas into reality with this book, made sure we met our deadlines, and never compromised on our vision.

Since I first moved to Atlanta more than twenty years ago, I have been amazed by the support from the design community. The love and appreciation for beautiful design in the South has been a true inspiration to me, and I am so appreciative to ADAC and everyone in our design community. Especially to my friend Dennis Hunt who has been an important part of my design world. Thank you for continuing to be such an inspiration and positive part of our whole, exciting evolution. And to Matthew Quinn, who is not only a talented and important part of our design team, but also a great friend.

Collaboration is one of the most rewarding aspects of every designer's work. Thank you to all of the talented architects. To me, it really is all about the architecture, and working together is my favorite part of the process. Thank you to the photographers who help bring my vision to reality and document all we do. To all the contractors, artisans, and workrooms that work with me to create beauty, you have my sincerest thanks. To Willard Pitt, my curtain maker for all these years, I am so grateful.

To all the editors and publications who have helped bring my work to a wider audience, thank you for your continuing support over all these years. My success would not be what it is today without all of you.

Charles Miers, Sandy Gilbert Freidus, and the entire team at Rizzoli, you have my deepest gratitude for your ongoing belief in me, your incredible encouragement and focus, and your admirable attention to detail.

To Jill Cohen, my friend of more than a decade, thank you for your support, guidance, and endless sage advice. My world is so much better having you in it. Your friendship means everything to me.

Thank you, Judith Nasatir, for capturing my voice and helping me find the words to share my message in a way that doesn't just express my design thoughts but also helps me to inspire others.

Doug Turshen and David Huang, a special thanks to you both for your incredible talents and for your fabulous ability to translate my work onto these pages in a way that truly reflects my sensibility and style.

To my licensing partners and associates, Hickory Chair, Visual Comfort, Ballard Designs, Lee Jofa, and La Cornue, I am truly grateful for our collaborations, which encourage me to be my best.

To my amazing clients, you inspire me. Working with you, I continue to grow and learn. Because of you, I am inspired to do my best work, and together, we create memories and very special homes.

And to my incredible family, the most special thank you of all: My husband, John Morris, my daughter, Alexandra Morris, Ashley Hurley, Ryan Morris, and my brother and sister, Jim and Nanette Kasler. You give me the freedom to reach places I never knew I could.

PHOTOGRAPHY

Peter Vitale: 2–3, 83–85, 87–95, 97–105

Douglas Friedman: 5, 8, 107, 109–127

Steve Pyle: 11

INSPIRED COLLAGE page 12
(left to right from top row) Brian Bieder, Emily Followill, Brian Bieder, Brian Bieder, Erica George Dines, Emily Followill, Phillip Ennis, Emily Followill, Brian Bieder

Phillip Ennis: Cover, 15–18

Emily Followill Photography: 20–21, 22

Brian Bieder Photography: 25–27, 29

TOWN COLLAGE page 30
(left to right from top row) Simon Upton, Simon Upton, Erica George Dines, Erica George Dines, Erica George Dines, Erica George Dines, Douglas Friedman, Peter Vitale

Simon Upton: 33, 35–43, 45, 46–51, 53, 56–59, 210, 213–221, 223–246, 249–250, 252–255, 257, 258, 260–261, 262–272

Mali Azima: 54–55

Erica George Dines: 61–62, 64–74, 76–81, 164, 167–183, 191, 274, 277–283, 285–301

COUNTRY COLLAGE page 128
(left to right from top row) William Waldron, William Waldron, Erica George Dines, Erica George Dines, William Waldron, Erica George Dines, Erica George Dines

William Waldron: 131, 135–140, 142–146, 149, 151–157, 159–163

Brian Vanden Brink: 132–133

Bjorn Wallander/OTTO: 185, 187–190, 192–197, 199–201, 203–205, 207

SHORE COLLAGE page 209
(left to right from top row) Simon Upton, Erica George Dines, Erica George Dines, Shane Carter Photography, Simon Upton, Simon Upton, Simon Upton

ARCHITECTURE

TOWN

BELLE MEADE
Architect: Renovations by Studio Eight Design, original architect Warterfield Goodwin Associates
Landscape architect: Page | Duke

BUCKHEAD
Architect: Spitzmiller & Norris
Landscape architect: E. Graham Pittman & Associates

ST. JAMES
Architect: Ruard Veltman Architecture
Landscape architect: Wertimer + Cline, Landscape Architects

TUXEDO
Architect: Harrison Design
Landscape architect: Land Plus Associates

COUNTRY

PORT CLYDE
Architect: Cole & Cole Architects
Landscape architect: Mohr & Seredin Landscape Architects

PALMETTO BLUFF
Architect: Pursley Dixon Architecture Inc.
Landscape architect: Witmer-Jones-Keefer, Ltd.

CANTERBURY
Architect: Madison Spencer Architects
Landscape architect: Rieley and Associates

SHORE

SEA ISLAND
Architect: Thomas Thaddeus Truett Architect
Landscape architect: Alex Smith Garden Design

NAPLES
Architect: Herscoe Hajjar Architects, Inc.
Landscape architect: Robin Renfroe

WATERCOLOR
Architect: Tammy Massey Architect
Landscape architect: Timeless Landscapes

First published in the United States of America in 2018
by Rizzoli International Publications, Inc.
300 Park Avenue South
New York, New York 10010
www.rizzoliusa.com

2019 2020 2021 2022/10 9 8 7 6 5 4 3 2

Printed in Italy

ISBN 13: 978-0-8478-6325-9

Library of Congress Control Number: 2018944468

Project Editor: Sandra Gilbert Freidus
Production: Maria Pia Gramaglia
Editorial assistance provided by Sara Pozefsky,
Kelli Rae Patton, and Rachel Selekman
Art Direction: Doug Turshen with David Huang
Endpapers: Cannes Print, Suzanne Kasler for Lee Jofa